Letterland

Handwriting
Practice 3

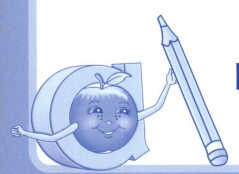

My name is _____ .

I am _____ years old.

Using this book

There are 52 basic letter shapes in written English (aA-zZ) and they are all abstract shapes. In Letterland these abstract shapes are bonded with child-friendly concrete images that act as memory cues. When your child sees the Letterland characters linked to the letter shapes, the risk of confusing all these abstract shapes is greatly reduced.

Correct formation ensures that the letters begin and end in the right place. This is especially important when your child is doing joined up (cursive) handwriting.
In this book they will review the first stages of joining letters (adding 'flick-ups') on pages 6-9 (for more on pre-cursive style, see **Handwriting Practice 2**). They will then go on to join all the letter shapes.

Pages 14-43 allow children to write many high usage words and words they will often come across in their daily lives. Use these pages in any order you prefer.
1) Read and discuss the message in the speech bubble.
(Note: in some words the characters will not be making their usual sounds. For stories to explain the new sounds, please look out for **Letterland Beyond ABC** and **Far Beyond ABC** Books.)
2) Create the letter stroke by overwriting the hollow letters in the top row.
3) Practice the join by making air strokes several times just over the black letters.
4) Overwrite the dash letter words.
5) Write the word as many more times as space allows.
6) Say the words as you write them.

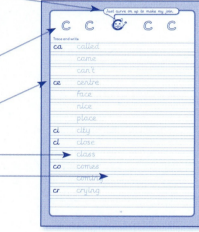

It is important to use this book:
  ✔ when your child is not tired
  ✔ when there are no background distractions, such as TV
  ✔ for short periods of time (ten minutes will probably be enough at first)
  ✔ with plenty of praise and encouragement.

Note: Some schools use different handwriting styles to this book. It is important to check which style your child's school uses.

Correct Handwriting Positions

Left-hander

Finger tips 4cm from tip of pencil

Paper side edge
30
Table Edge

Elbows off the table

Right-hander

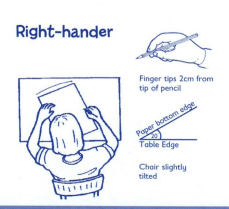

Finger tips 2cm from tip of pencil

Paper bottom edge
20
Table Edge

Chair slightly tilted

Contents

Warm up!

Trace

4

Small letters

Trace and write

 a   a   a   a

 c   c   c   c

 e   e   e   e

 i   i   i   i

 m   m   m   m

 n   n   n   n

 o   o   o   o

Trace and write

r   r   r   r   r

s   s   s   s   s

u   u   u   u   u

v   v   v   v   v

w   w   w   w   w

x   x   x   x   x

z   z   z   z   z

Tall letters

Trace and write

b   b   b   b

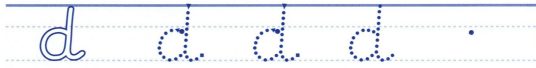

d   d   d   d

h   h   h   h

k   k   k   k

l   l   l   l

t   t   t   t

f   f   f   f

Descenders

Trace and write

 g   g   g   g   g

 j   j   j   j   j

 p   p   p   p   p

 q   q   q   q   q

 y   y   y   y   y

Let's join — 12 letters join up from the base line.

a a a   and

          animal

c c c   can

          came

d d d   daddy

e e e   eating

i i i   inside

m m m   might

n n n   nine

u u u   uncle

h h   k k   l l   t t

hand kite like ten

Let's join - Five letters join up along the top.

f f	for
	from
o o	old
r r	road
v v	visit
w w	word

'Break' letters — Eight letters are 'break' letters.

b p s g j

rabbit   puppy   hiss

giggle   jump

x y z q

extra   yo-yos

whizzing   quick

Join lines

a a a a a   b b b b

c c c c   d d d d

e e e e   f f f

g g g g   h h h h h

i u u i   j j j j

k k k k   l l l l

m m m m   n n n

o o o o o

p p p p

qu qu qu

r r r r

s s s s

t t t t

u u u u u

v v v v

w w w w

x x x x

y y y y

z z z z

No exit strokes for b, f, g, j, p, s, x, y or z.

Turn my flick-up into a join.

a   a   **a**   a   a

Trace and write

ab	about
ac	across
af	after
ag	again
ai	air
al	almost
	always
am	among
an	another
ar	any
	are
as	ask
au	aunt
aw	away

b   b   b   b   b

Remember I'm a 'break' letter.

Trace and write

ba   baby

back

bang

be   because

before

behind

bi   bird

birthday

bl   black

bo   boat

book

br   brother

bu   but

building

C   C   C   C   C

Trace and write

ca   called

came

can't

ce   centre

face

nice

place

ci   city

cl   close

class

co   comes

coming

cr   crying

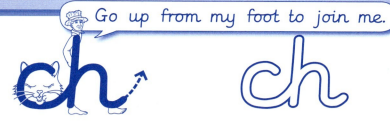

Go up from my foot to join me.

Trace and write

ch   ch   ch   ch

chair

cheek

child

choose

chose

church

such

teacher

d d **d** d d

Draw my join like this.

Trace and write

da   day
      dark

de   dear
      decide

di   did
      didn't
      die

do   don't
      done
      door
      down

dr   dress
      drink

du   during

Trace and write

ea	each
	easy
	eat
	ear
	early
eg	egg
ei	eight
en	end
	enough
ev	even
	every
	everything
ex	except
ey	eye

f   f   f   f   f

Cross my letter before you move on.

Trace and write

fa   father

      family

fe   felt

      few

fi   fine

      first

      fire

fl   floor

      flower

fo   for

      four

fr   friend

      from

fu   funny

g   g   g   g   g

It's good to take a break after my letter.

Trace and write

ga	game
	garden
	gave
ge	get
	getting
gi	girls
	give
gl	glad
	glasses
go	goes
	going
gr	grass
	great
gu	guess

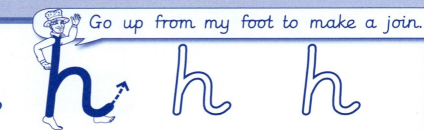

h h **h** h h

Trace and write

ha	happen
	hasn't
	hard
he	help
	head
hi	high
ho	how
	horse
	house
	hour
hu	hunt
	hurt
-ht	right
	eight

i i i i i

Finish the word. Then dot my letter.

Trace and write

if	if
in	into
	invite
it	itself
	it's
is	isn't
I'll	I'll
I've	I've

25

j j j j j

Same here! Don't forget I'm a 'break' letter.

Trace and write

ja   jam

je   jeans

            jelly

jo   job

            joy

ju   just

            jumped

k k k k k

Turn my flick-up into a kick-up.

Trace and write

ke	keep
	kept
ki	kill
	killed
	kind
	king
	kite
	kitten
kn	know
	knows
	known
	knew
kni	knife
	knives

27

l l l l l

Start my join where my dress flicks up.

Trace and write

la   lake

last

large

le   left

letter

li   life

light

little

liked

lived

lo   long

looked

lots

lu   lunch

m m m m m

Make my flick-up into a join.

Trace and write

ma made

many

me men

meat

mi milk

might

min mine

minute

mo money

month

mor more

morning

mu mummy

my myself

n n n n n

Trace and write

na name

named

ne near

nearly

neck

never

next

ni nice

night

nine

no nose

noses

nothing

now

You'll be using my top joins most.

Trace and write

o'c   o'clock

oi   oil

on   only

       on

       one

       once

op   opened

       opening

or   orange

       order

ou   our

       outside

ov   over

ow   own

Here's my special join next to e.

Trace and write

oe   goes

          does

          toes

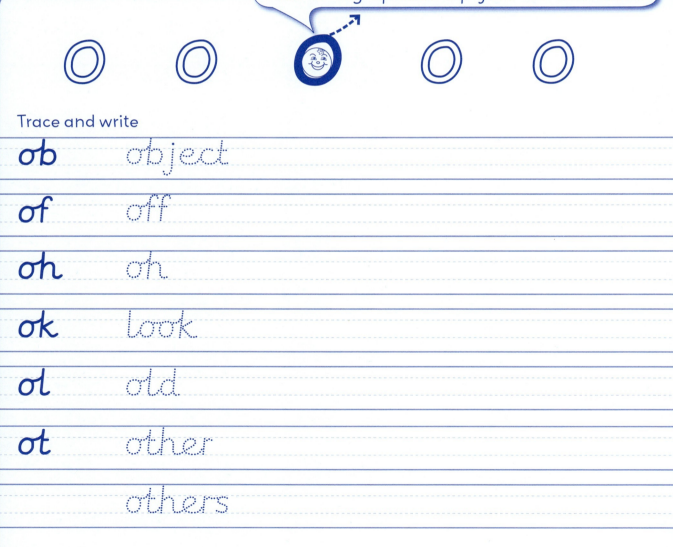

This is my special top join for tall letters.

Trace and write

ob   object

of   off

oh   oh

ok   look

ol   old

ot   other

          others

p p p p p

Remember, please, I'm a 'break' letter.

Trace and write

pa   pair

      paper

par   park

      party

pe   pencil

      people

pi   picture

      piece

pl   plan

      please

po   poor

pr   present

      pretty

pu   put

33

qu

Join us quickly. I insist!

qu

Trace and write

qu	queen
qua	quarter
qui	quick
	quickly
	quiet

u

u   u   u   u

Turn my flick-up into a join.

Trace and write

un	under
	until
	uncle
up	upon
us	use
	used
	using

r r r r r

Trace and write

ra rabbit

radio

raced

racing

rained

re real

rest

ready

ri ride

riding

right

river

ro road

room

Remember I'm a 'break' letter.

S   S   S   S   S

Trace and write

sa	said
	says
sc	schools
se	seconds
	seven
si	since
sk	skips
sl	sleeps
sm	smallest
sn	snows
so	sometimes
sp	spell
st	starts
sw	swims

Sammy is a 'break' letter, but I am not.

sh　sh　sh

Trace and write

sh　sh　sh　sh

shall

she

shine

shoe

shop

should

shout

shut

dish

fish

wash

splash

t t t t t

Trace and write

ta	table
	take
te	tenth
	tell
	teacher
ti	time
to	together
	told
	tooth
	town
tr	train
	tree
	trip
tu	turn

th th th

Trace and write

tha   than

that

thank

the   then

there

they

them

their

thi   this

thing

think

tho   those

thought

thr   through

Start your join at my vase edge.

V   V   V   V   V

Trace and write

ve	very
vi	visit
	visiting
	visited

Take a break after you write my letter.

y   y   y   y   y

Trace and write

ya	yard
ye	yet
	yellow
	yesterday
yo	you
	yours
	young

W   W   W   W   W

Trace and write

wa   walk

wasn't

watch

water

we   wear

were

weren't

wi   wish

without

wh   wh   wh

Trace and write

wh   what

          when

          where

          why

          while

wh   wh   wh

wh   who

wh   whose

I like being a 'break' letter.

Trace and write

ax	axe
ex	except
	excuse
ix	fix
ox	fox

I'm the last 'break' letter.

Trace and write

az	lazy
ez	freeze
iz	size
zo	zoo

Capital letters

All the capitals letters start at the top.

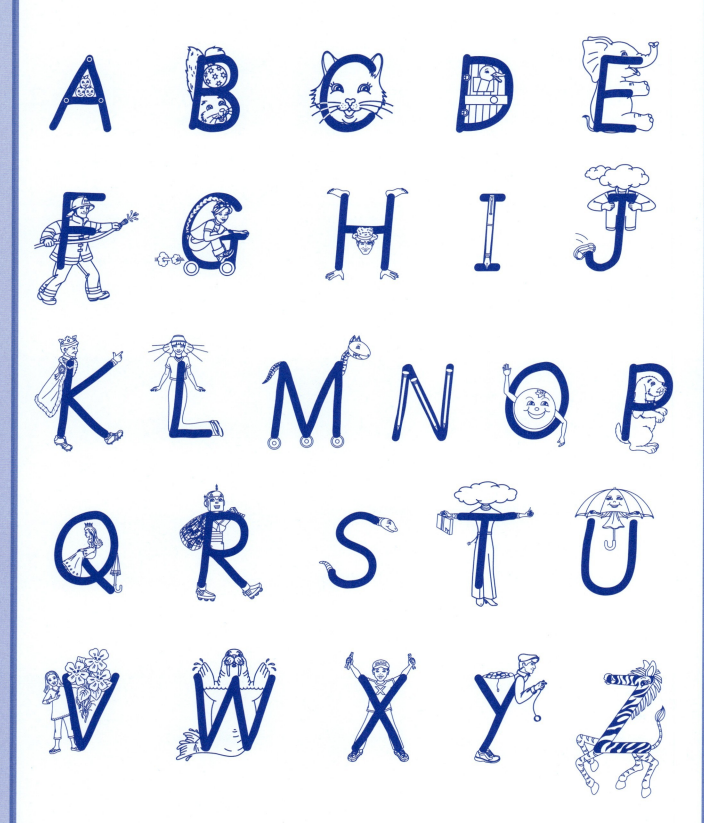

Aa Bb Cc Dd Ee

Ff Gg Hh Ii Jj

Kk Ll Mm Nn Oo

Pp Qq Rr Ss Tt

Uu Vv Ww Xx Yy Zz

Signs

Do not join the capital letters but keep them close.

Trace and write

Airport	A
Caution	C
Closed	C
DANGER	D
Dentist	D
Doctor	D
Emergency	E
EXIT	E
Fire Escape	F
Hospital	H
Information	I
Inquiries	I
Junior School	J
Keep Out	K

Library	L
No Smoking	N
Nursery	N
Open	O
Parking	P
Please Pay Here	P
Queue Here	Q
Reception	R
Station	S
STOP	S
Swimming Pool	S
Telephone	T
Thank you	T
Toilet	T
Welcome	W
Zoo	Z

Colours

Trace, write and colour

red

yellow

blue

green

pink

purple

brown

orange

black

white

The colour I like the

most is _____

Days of the week

Trace and write

Monday

Tuesday

Wednesday

Thursday

Friday

Saturday

Sunday

Numbers

one	seven
two	eight
three	nine
four	ten
five	eleven
six	twelve

Months of the year

Trace and write

January

February

March

April

May

June

July

August

September

October

November

December

My birthday is _____

Writing an invitation

Dear _____

You are invited to my birthday party on _____

at _____

Love from

_____

Left-handers

You may prefer to cross to the left.

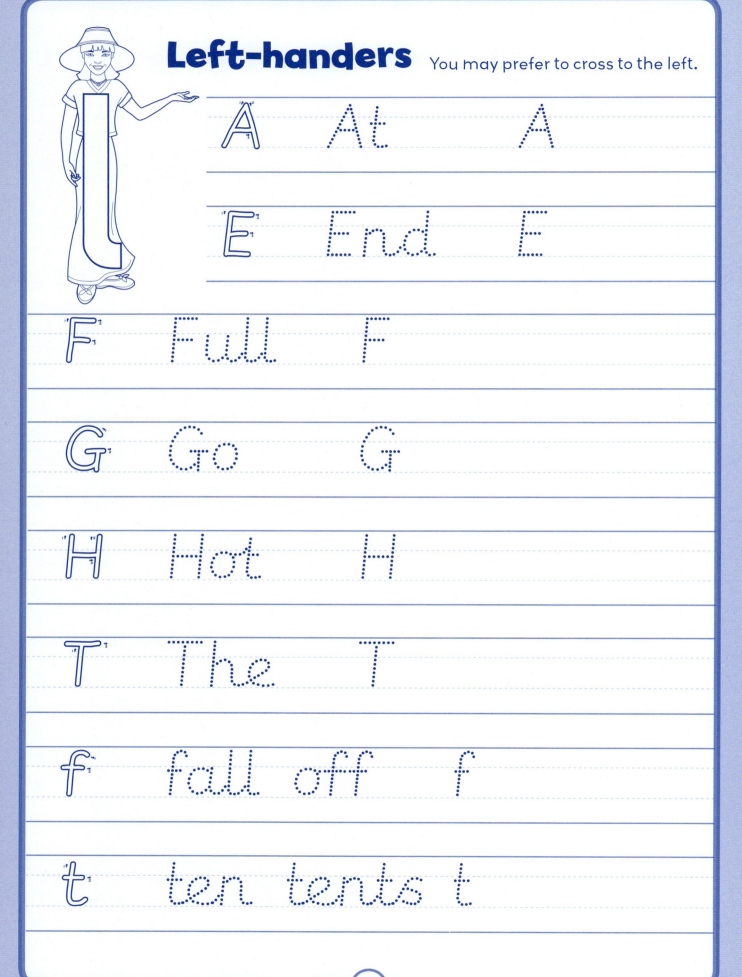

A   At   A

E   End   E

F   Full   F

G   Go   G

H   Hot   H

T   The   T

f   fall off   f

t   ten tents   t

Lined practice pages

Letterlanders

Annie Apple   Bouncy Ben   Clever Cat   Dippy Duck   Eddy Elephant   Firefighter Fred   Golden Girl

Harry Hat Man   Impy Ink   Jumping Jim   Kicking King   Lucy Lamp Light   Munching Mike

Noisy Nick   Oscar Orange   Peter Puppy   Quarrelsome Queen   Red Robot   Sammy Snake

Talking Tess   Uppy Umbrella   Vicky Violet   Walter Walrus   Fix-it Max   Yellow Yo-yo Man   Zig Zag Zebra